Jack McArdle

The Higher Power

the columba press

the columba press

93 The Rise, Mount Merrion, Blackrock, Co Dublin, Ireland

First edition 1988
Cover by Bill Bolger
Origination by Typeform Ltd, Dublin
Printed in Ireland by
Genprint Ltd, Dublin

ISBN 0 948183 63 2

Contents

Introduction

This book is one that I am trying to *live*. It is more personal than anything I have ever written. I cannot write about Christian living without reference to theology that is both basic and profound. What I have attempted to do, however, is to provide a new theological language. This may *sound* pretentious, but it is not intended to be. I have always believed that there just *has* to be a simpler way of stating Gospel truths, and this is one such way.

If a theologian is one who knows something about God, then a person who prays is a theologian. When it comes to the truths of the Gospel, then 'flesh and blood cannot reveal them' (Mt 16:17). And when it comes to speaking the truths of the Gospel 'you will be given what to say, for it will not be you speaking, but the Spirit of your Father speaking through you' (Mt 10:20).

The journey outlined in this book is one in which I travel, fail, fall, and start again, every day of my life. I have pondered, prayed and shared these truths again and again. I believe that what is most human is most universal, and I believe that the reader will recognise many of the road-signs along the way, and may find encouragement in the recognition.

With Paul 'I pray that the eyes of your hearts may be enlightened in order that you may know the hope to which he has called you . . . and his incomparably great power for us who believe. That power is like the working of his mighty strength, which he exerted in Christ . . . .' (Eph 1:18-19). If, like me, you exhausted human power again and again, in the struggle with human weaknesses, then you, too, may be better prepared, and more open to handing the task over to a Higher Power!

CHAPTER ONE

The raisins in the dough

The raisins in the dough

Nobody could ever make bread like my mother! There was no measuring; a fist of this, a pinch of that, and a sprinkle of the other – and it always came out perfect. It was *always* special when I saw the currants or raisins to hand – and she was generous with them as well.

Now supposing I compare our *human nature* to that dough that is ready for the oven, it may help us to understand ourselves a bit better. The problem, of course, with the 'dough' of our human nature is that it should have a government health warning on it! Our nature is contaminated because of the 'radio-active fall-out' of original sin, and there are elements in it that are not safe for human consumption – like fears, jealousies, laziness, etc. I often think of those imperfections or weaknesses as my mother's generous supply of raisins!

On occasions my mother would then take her rolling pin, flatten out the dough, and with a tumbler held upside-down, which she kept dipping into dry flour, she would divide up the dough into scones. Returning to the topic of our human nature, I am suggesting that each of us is one of those scones! Each scone is different, if from the one mix, and the allocation of imperfections is not exactly the same in any two. Some scones are bound to have more raisins than others, and just as the lines of a finger print are unique and special to each individual, so is the combination of human weaknesses.

One person is totally addictive and compulsive, and such a person will finish the box of chocolates, empty the bottle, and end up picking the skeleton of the chicken. His brother has never smoked in his life, is very intolerant of alcohol, and can never understand how anyone could eat between meals. Another experiences quite acute mood swings, hits air-pockets, and goes into nose-dives of depression on a regular basis, while her sister is always bubbling over, even on Monday mornings! A failure to understand and appreciate this essential uniqueness and difference of one person from another results in all judgements, which are always wrong. 'Do you know what that guy's after doing? Well, *I* certainly wouldn't do a thing like *that.*' And he's probably right, he wouldn't – because he does not have that weakness! It's even possible that God saw that he would be too weak to survive if he had to struggle with that imperfection!

It is generally accepted that if a group of people could possibly exchange weaknesses, that, within an hour, each would beg to get his own weaknesses back! God has 'wired' each of us in such a way that even my imperfections are tailor-made, and best suited to the person I am.

These weaknesses are not sin, of course. They are the result of sin, or original sin, not of my own sin. There is a very simple parable in Matthew's Gospel (13:24-30) that helps in our understanding of all this. A man sowed *good* seed in his field, but that night an *enemy* sowed weeds among the wheat. The workers were surprised to see the weeds, and when they asked the man he told them not to attempt to remove the weeds, because they would do more harm than good. He said that he himself would deal with the weeds when the proper time came.

The parallel is obvious. When God created human nature, 'He saw that it was good' (Gen 1:31). Then the enemy of God and man came under the cover of a lie and he succeeded in sowing the seeds of fear, darkness and death. 'An enemy has done this. Yes, the seed I sowed was good, and it still is. Let both grow together until the harvest, and I will sort things out at that time.'

At this stage it might be appropriate to mention something about self-acceptance. The idea is often put forward but I'm not sure if it is that well understood. Self-acceptance is to *know* what my imperfections are, and to agree that they are all mine! It is to know my strengths as well, of course, but for now I must limit the scope of the definition. Accepting is agreeing, not excusing or flaunting. I am neither ashamed nor proud of my imperfections; I just agree that I have them. When I know what they are and I acknowledge their presence, then the basic condition is there for doing something about them.

A frequent trap to fall into is comparing myself with someone else. I wish I had that person's weaknesses! I wouldn't really say it like that, but, I can recognise envy, jealousy, and a feeling of inferiority when I compare myself with others. On the other hand, the comparison can produce pride and self-righteousness. The Pharisee in the gospel (Lk 18:10-14) was telling God what his strengths and the Publican's weaknesses were! On the other hand, the Publican spoke for himself and about himself – and he was the one 'who went away justified'.

The Incarnation is about what Jesus did when he personally took on our human nature with *all* of its weaknesses and imperfections. All and any possibility of my facing up to my weaknesses stems directly from what Jesus did, and what he made possible for me. My starting point is to be as realistic as possible: to accept the different allocation of imperfections in each person; to acknowledge and to admit my own; – and to concede that I need a Higher Power if there is to be any success in opposing them.

CHAPTER TWO

A man with a mission

A man with a mission

Some people think of Jesus as anything but incarnate, as not real flesh and blood. They would have him sitting up in his carry-cot (without a soother!) looking out at all those people he was going to have to save later on! This image is false and very misleading to a proper understanding of why Jesus came and what he did when he came. Jesus spent the first thirty years of his life *listening,* which is a very good description of prayer. Prayer is not man talking to God who doesn't hear, but God talking to man who won't listen! After thirty years, Jesus knew what he had to do. In his own person he would take on all of the mix!

He headed for the Jordan river where John the Baptist was holding a rally for sinners. John was really taken aback when he spotted Jesus in the queue! But John tried to deter him, saying, 'I need to be baptised by you, and do you come to me?' (Mt 3:14). While perhaps not fully understanding, John at least had his suspicions as to who Jesus might be. John was a prophet and 'greater than a prophet' (Lk 7:26). He knew that Jesus did not need repentance and baptism for the forgiveness of sins like his other clients, but when Jesus told him, 'Let it be so now; it is proper for us to do this . . ' (Mt 3:15), he was enough of a prophet to get on with it, and question no more.

Jesus took the first great risk of his life when he came to the Jordan. He that was without sin was willing to become sin (Rom 8:3). He took on the whole burden of human weaknesses and imperfections. The risk involved was that, with such a burden on his shoulders, he would have sunk to the bottom of that river and never surfaced again! But what happened? What always happens when we take on, or help to carry, the burdens and brokenness of others: The Father gave the Power – the whole lot of it! The Spirit and Power of God descended upon Jesus in visible form, that's what happened. At the very moment he took on all of our human weaknesses and imperfections he also received all of the Power of God. The Father had not failed him, and he could speak with a passionate conviction of such a caring Father over the following three years.

Jesus had left his divinity to one side. 'He did not claim equality with God, but became like us in all things, except sin' (Phil 2:6). He took on all of our human weaknesses, but, of course, these weaknesses are not sin, but they can lead to sin. As he struggled with each of those weaknesses, one after another, he could challenge his critics: 'Who can accuse me of sin?' (Jn 8:46). He now had within him the power of God. The next three years would show just how that power was so much greater than all of human weaknesses. I have already said that Jesus had left his divinity to one side, as it were. It would be a mistake, then, to think that he worked miracles because he was God. No, he worked miracles because he had the power of God (Holy Spirit) within him. Later on, he would promise us the same power – and then, 'greater things will you do' (Jn 14:12).

Here we now have Jesus with all of human weaknesses and imperfections on his shoulders, and with the power of God within him. The lines are sharply drawn and the battle begins in earnest. In his own person he will now do battle and struggle with each and every human weakness, one after another. I'm not sure that this is too well understood. The cosmetic antiseptic Jesus of some people really never had a struggle or a problem! Such people seem to by-pass or gloss over such sentences in the gospel as 'He gave a deep groan . . ' (of frustration) (Mk 8:12). In actual *fact,* I could say to anybody: 'Think of *any* human weakness or imperfection – have you one in mind? – well Jesus had a *real* struggle on his hands in that very area.'

We get a glimpse of some of those struggles. He struggled with fear until he sweated blood (Lk 22:44). Immediately, of course, I must add that, with the power within him, he overcame that fear and did not run away. He struggled, yes, but 'who can accuse me of sin?' (Jn 8:46). The fact of the matter is that he spent many a night in many a garden facing up to, and struggling with every form of human weakness. His struggle in Gethsemane is described as prayer: 'Sit here while I go over there and *pray* . .; He left them, went away, and *prayed* the third time . .' (Mt 26:36,44). He even gives them a hint as to the nature of the struggle, and the formula for victory: *'Watch and pray* that you do not fall into temptation' (Mt 26:41).

There are many references in the gospel when one might well suspect a struggle to be going on within him: 'After he had sent the people away, he went up a hill by himself to pray' (Mt 14:23). 'He went out of the town to a lonely place, where he prayed' (Mk 1:35). 'But he would go away to lonely places, where he prayed' (Lk 5:16). '. . . and spent the whole night there praying to God' (Jn 6:12). I personally suspect that there may well have been a sweat of blood during these sessions also.

Jesus was accused of being a glutten and a drunkard (Lk 7:34) – and I have no doubt that there was some foundation for the accusation! I am not saying that Jesus ever got drunk, or ever ate to excess. What I am saying is that he liked food and he liked a drink, and he had to challenge and restrain these appetites to keep them in check. He would have had the same problems with diets as the rest of us! He would have had the same problems, but would have had a much better track record, and more consistent success. He came both *'to do'* and *'to teach'* (Acts 1:1), and before he would ask any of us to let our 'yes' be *yes* (Mt 5:37), he certainly would have done so himself.

It is essential to remind ourselves of the 'Power Within' when we speak of Jesus. When the power is external it is suppression and repression, and when it is within it is discipline. When I speak of Christianity in a later chapter I will be stressing that it is really about what happens *within,* and the external behaviour, and code of conduct, flows automatically from that.

When Jesus was tempted by Satan in the desert, it does not necessarily mean that Jesus sat on one sand dune and Satan on another, and they were having a conversation. No, he was genuinely tempted just like you and me. Satan spots the weakness, and he dangles a temptation in front of it, that has the effect of a magnet on metal filings. Jesus was experiencing the surge of power within him after his baptism in the Jordan. One could easily be tempted to try out that new power with a stones-to-bread trick, or a reckless leap from a height, and trust one's inner power to come to the rescue! Jesus promised his disciples that they could 'pick up snakes with their hands, and when they drink deadly poison, it will not hurt them at all' (Mk 16:18). Some of his 'disciples' (sic) in Colorado did just that a few years back – and they died! Dealing with such temptations Jesus would consult the Father's word, and as he spoke that word with the power of the Spirit, the Tempter was put to flight. Once again I stress that Jesus could do this, not because he was God, but because he had the power of God in him. That self-same power would be made available to his disciples when he himself had completed his own personal victory.

When I say that Jesus had to struggle with *every* human weakness, then the 'followers' of 'Good old plastic Jesus' would have a real problem with me! When I suggest that he could have had a real struggle on his hands in dealing with his relationship with Mary Magdalene I might well be accused of blasphemy! Of course he was capable of a very pure unselfish love, and did, in fact, have that kind of love for her, and for the many other 'groupies' who flocked around him and were drawn to him. They loved him, it was obvious, and he certainly loved them. What I am saying is that this was not easy for him, and were it not for his Inner Power it would have proved impossible.

In *Jesus Christ, Superstar* Mary Magdalene sings 'I don't know how to love him.' My understanding of the situation is that Jesus could reply 'At the beginning I didn't know how to love you either, but as I listened to the voice of the Father within, I *learned* how to love you – and now I *really* love you.' He was accused of consorting with such people, and of attracting them. 'If he were a prophet, he would surely know who is touching him, and what kind of woman she is – that she is a sinner' (Lk 7:39). At his trial he would assert that he had always acted openly for all to see (Jn 18:20). Of course, on a human level, it would be impossible to believe that there was no sin involved – because, on a human level it would have been impossible! 'You make judgements in a purely human way' he told his accusers (Jn 8:15). 'Stop judging by external standards' he told them (Jn 7:24). And again, he said that those who have a worldly mind-set 'are wrong about judgement' (Jn 16:11). The more I examine this whole area, the more convinced I am that it must have been really difficult to be Jesus!

I can summarise this chapter by saying that if there is

any weakness in you or me that Jesus did not personally encounter, struggle with and overcome — then we are not saved! It is because of what Jesus *did* in his own personal life that I have any hope in mine. Incarnation meant taking on all of human nature, including mine. 'For we do not have a High Priest who is unable to sympathise with our weaknesses, but we have one who has been tempted *in every way*, just as we are — yet was without sin' (Heb 4:15).

CHAPTER THREE

The final hurdle

The final hurdle

When the new-born baby is first held and welcomed in the labour ward, there can flood in a whole series of questions, speculations, and uncertainties about the future. The child could be a Pope one day, or a murderer; a great artist, or totally autistic. All we can do is hope, speculate, and dream. Only one thing is certain: *he will die*. That is the one weakness that is shared by every human being. As I write the word 'human', I could write in brackets after it 'and therefore limited, finite, and mortal – destined to die'. As far as Jesus was concerned 'the final enemy was death' (1 Cor 15:26).

Once Jesus realised that he had to go all the way in the struggle he took on, that he had to 'become obedient even onto death' (Phil 2:8), he set his face firmly and resolutely towards Jerusalem (Mt 16:21). In fact one senses a restlessness and an impatience within him to bring the struggle to a conclusion. Again, it was not easy, but once again his Inner Power brought him safely through. Even in himself, he could experience that the Spirit was willing but the flesh was weak and afraid (Mk 14:38). Of all his struggles with all of human weaknesses, this final struggle is the one that is best chronicled in the gospel. We can chart the journey from the time when he slipped into Jerusalem on his own, taking normal precautions against being arrested (Jn 7:10), to the time when, with his last breath, he reminded the Father that his task was now completed (Jn 19:30).

In the garden, we see Jesus coming to grips with the whole concept of death, and later on with the reality. We all know that we *have* to die, but we're never too sure what to do about it. Should we face up to it now and live with that reality, or should we wait until it approaches us? 'But I have a baptism to undergo, and how distressed I am until it is completed' (Lk 12:50). It would seem that Jesus always kept this final struggle in mind, and I'm sure he saw it as the greatest struggle of all.

There is one dimension of his death, however, that must be stressed. His whole life was a constant dying. He 'did not consider equality with God something to be grasped, but made himself nothing, taking the very nature of a servant, being made in human likeness' (Phil 2:6-7). His life was a constant dying to self. On the cross, when he had every reason to wallow in self-pity, he showed concern for his mother, his friend John, a man on a cross beside him, and he even prayed for those who were killing him. That was the real dying.

I said in an earlier chapter that Jesus spent many a night in many a garden struggling with human weaknesses. During this final struggle with the final enemy, we have, as it were, a ring-side seat. Dying is not something that *happens* to me; it is something I have to *do*. It is a passage or a journey that I have to undergo *alone*. It has its own unique aloneness and loneliness. Jesus had the extra pain of knowing that the only one of his apostles who was awake and alert that night was Judas, because there was money in it for him! Judas was the only one to kiss him that night! 'I looked for sympathy but there was none, for comforters, but I found none' (Ps 69:20).

His 'very meat was to do the will of him who sent him' (Jn 4:34), and, therefore, he always had an 'open line' to the Father in prayer. 'Being in anguish, he prayed more earnestly' (Lk 22:44). While struggling with a human weakness he made sure that he was 'plugged into' divine strength. His prayer was not some sort of anaesthetic. He also needed to be fully alert – to 'watch and pray' (Mt

26:41). Satan can slip in through the slightest chink in our armour. In fact he had tried unsuccessfully to prevent Jesus from going near Jerusalem in the first instance. When he told his disciples what was going to happen to him in Jerusalem 'he spoke plainly about this, and Peter took him aside and began to rebuke him. But when Jesus turned and looked at his disciples *he rebuked Peter.* 'Out of my sight, Satan!' he said. 'You do not have in mind the things of God, but the things of man' (Mk 8:31-33).

Jesus took his first great risk when he went down into the river Jordan with the burden of all human weaknesses and imperfections on his back. He took his second great risk when he bowed his head in death. And once again the Father proved that he could be trusted. The Father 'caught' him, as it were, and brought him safely through death into the fullness of life. In human terms it was a close call! It was a close call for us as well as for Jesus. 'And if Christ has not been raised, your faith is futile; you are still in your sins. Then those who have fallen asleep in Christ are lost' (1 Cor 15:17-18). If he failed in this final struggle, he would be like a horse-show rider with a faultless round until he came crashing through the final hurdle!

Christ's victory was now complete. 'Death has been swallowed up in victory.' 'Where, O death is your victory? Where, O death, is your sting?' (1 Cor 15:54-55). Christ had overcome death, and, for the Christian, it is no longer an enemy.

Christ overcame sin. Sin enters in through human weaknesses and imperfections, but in Christ sin had failed to gain access. 'Who can accuse me of sin?' (Jn 8:46). He was the Lamb of God who came to take away the sins of the world (Jn 1:29). Before he could be an antidote for sin in our lives he had to do battle with sin, and have his own personal victory over it. Satan dangles the temptation to sin outside the windows of our weaknesses, but Jesus exposed him for the lying and deceitful salesman that he is, and now 'the prince of this world stands condemned' (Jn 16:11).

Jesus overcame sickness. He made a very clear distinction between sickness and suffering. He showed in both word and act that the struggle against human weaknesses must involve suffering: 'anyone who does not take up his cross and follow me is not worthy of me' (Mt 10:38). 'If anyone would come after me, he must deny himself, and take up his cross daily, and follow me' (Lk 9:23). The suffering that is essential to the struggle is at the very heart of Christian living. Suffering may often include some form of sickness, but not all sickness is suffering. Sickness is not necessarily from God. Enough alcohol and enough nicotine – and don't blame God for what happens to your liver or your lungs! 'Is any one of you sick? He should call the elders of the church to pray over him and anoint him with oil in the name of the Lord. And their prayer offered in faith will make the sick person well; the Lord will raise him up. If he has sinned, he will be forgiven' (Jas 5:14-15).

Jesus had taken on the complete 'mix', and through total obedience to the Father, continual reliance on the inner power of the Spirit, and unselfish acceptance of each personal struggle, he had won through to the end. 'During the days of Jesus' life on earth, he offered up prayers and petitions with loud cries and tears to the one who could save him from death, and he was heard because of his reverent submission. Although he was a son, he *learned* obedience from what he suffered, and, once made perfect, he became the source of eternal salvation for all who obey him. (Heb 5:7-9).

23

CHAPTER FOUR

Another Christ

Another Christ

Still retaining the idea of the mix for the brown bread, let us now see what happens after Jesus obtained the victory. We roll out the dough again, and we return to the scones once more. Imagine your surprise and disappointment when you examine the scone you receive, and find the very same weaknesses there that you would have had if Jesus had never come! It is often accepted that Jesus came *to take away* our weaknesses. This is not true. Having personally overcome and reduced to submission *all* of human weaknesses through the power of his inner Spirit, he *showed* us what could be done. He then returns the scone to us with our four or five rebellious inclinations, offers us the very same Spirit with which he overcame the lot – and he says, 'Now, *you* get on with it! It's your turn now to do on a minor scale what I did on the total scale.'

When I think of our mission in comparison with his, I have a mental image that helps me see the heart of the connection. It is of a little girl in junior school who had her photograph taken in school. She comes home to Mammy, all excited, with one large photograph and two small ones. The large photograph represents Jesus, and one of the small ones represents me. It is the *same picture* on a smaller scale.

When Jesus went down into the Jordan river he took all of our human weaknesses upon his shoulders. It was an act of total love for us, and of obedience to the Father. It was then, at that very moment, that he received *all* of the power of God. I, too, must go down into that river with him. I must personally accept and acknowledge the weaknesses and imperfections that I find in my share-out of human nature. These imperfections are not sin; they are the result of sin, of someone else's sin, of original sin. When I willingly accept those weaknesses and the necessary struggle that must be mine because of them, I *then* receive the power and Spirit of God to do battle with them and against them. It is a great temptation to want to be rid of them; to imagine that there's something wrong with me because of them; or to think of any effort to deal with them as hopeless and doomed to failure.

There is one point that must be emphasised again and again: by myself I can do nothing about them! If I put my foot up on a stool and begin to saw off my leg above the knee I don't think I would succeed! My leg is part of me, and the task would be impossible! Supposing I did succeed however, I would still have my weaknesses – because they are more part of me than my leg! For me, with human endeavour, to attempt to do anything to change and improve my human nature is like adding water to water and expecting to get a stronger drink! The strength just *has* to be God's. This is something that the Holy Spirit alone can do.

Let me make a distinction here to help clarify something that sometimes puzzles people. Jesus came down on this earth, did all he came to do, and then he went back home, and put up his feet! 'He now sits at the right hand of the Father' (Creed). He then turned to the Holy Spirit, as if to say 'C'mon 'tis your turn now!' He sent the Holy Spirit . . . to complete his work on earth, and to bring us the fullness of grace' (Eucharistic Prayer 4). It is the Holy Spirit who gets things done around here, especially when it comes to changing hearts. Of course, we pray to Jesus, and we pray to the Father, but when it comes to the power we need in our daily struggles with our weaknesses, then the Holy Spirit is that power.

I bring a group to the Holy Land in the month of

October every year. We go out there to pray and to ponder in the very places in which Jesus struggled. We spend varying times in Gethsemane, on Calvary, in the desert, or on the hillsides of Galilee. These are the places that were his arena. At the end of our Retreat it is hoped that each member of the group will return home with the conviction: 'For *me*, the Holy Land is in my heart. That's where my Bethlehem, Nazareth, Calvary, Easter and Pentecost have to take place. I need not have gone all the way to Israel after all!'

Life on earth is a warfare, a constant battle between what I *ought* to do and what 'I'd *love* to do. Our struggle is the same as that of Jesus. 'In your struggle against sin, you have not yet resisted to the point of shedding your blood' (Heb 12:4). I may never be asked to sweat blood or to shed blood, but the struggle is just as real. The fact that our weaknesses are so much part of us that they have an entrenched position within us, and can never be trusted. No one should ever say 'I *was* an alcoholic', because, even if he has not taken a drink for thirty years, he *is* an alcoholic, and will be an alcoholic until the day he dies. Even when inactive, our weaknesses are like sleeping giants that are stirred into activity at the slightest provocation. When the enemy (Satan) dangles his wares outside the windows of our weaknesses, he knows that there is a fifth column within us only too ready and willing to open the gates and let him in. '*Watch* and pray so that you will not fall into temptation. The spirit is willing but the flesh is weak' (Mk 14:38).

CHAPTER FIVE

The Higher Power

The Higher Power

There are many false notions about Christianity. It is sometimes seen as producing nicer people with better morals – a wholly external performance job! It is also seen as trying to live as Christ lived by imitating (or mimicking?) him. Both view-points are essentially misleading.

If producing nicer people with better morals was the purpose, then I could remain a pagan and still qualify! Using this criterion, then Jesus should have been very pleased with the Pharisees, who were so correct and proper – on the outside. However, this is the very thing that Jesus condemned most forcefully. 'Woe to you, teachers of the law and Pharisees, you hypocrites! You clean the *outside* of the cup and dish, but inside they are full of greed and self-indulgence. Blind Pharisee! First clean the *inside* of the cup and dish, and then the outside also will be clean . . . You are like whitewashed tombs, which look beautiful on the outside, but on the inside are full of dead men's bones and everything unclean. In the same way, on the outside you appear to people as righteous, but on the inside you are full of hypocrisy and wickedness' (Mt 23:25-28). So much for external behaviour and appearances that is unconnected with the heart within!

If Christianity were about prayer and fasting, then Muslims would be excellent Christians, because their schedule for times and places of prayer and their month long fasting on special occasions would prove an impossible standard for the average Christian!

Christianity is about what happens inside, and then the

external behaviour automatically falls into line. 'I will remove from them their hearts of stone and give them a heart of flesh. I will give them an undivided heart and put a new spirit in them' (Ezek 11:19-20). 'These people honour me with their lips but their hearts are far from me' (Mk 7:6). The organ God gave me to pray with is my *heart,* not my *tongue.* If the heart is not praying, then the tongue is wasting its time!

Quite often there is no connection between the external behaviour and the heart. I could meet you, and ask you how you are – but please don't answer, because inside I really don't want to know! Many expressions of concern, of sympathy, of support, or of well-wishing could be hollow and meaningless because they are not coming from *within.*

Christianity is all about a change of heart. It is about God's Spirit entering in there just as truly as happened to Jesus at the Jordan river. It then means that I give witness, through the weakensses, of having that Higher Power within. It is certainly not about imitating Jesus. It is about doing exactly what he did – made possible through dependence and reliance on the same Power. It means that with this Power, 'even greater things than this will I do' (Jn 5:10). It means being raised by a Higher Power to a higher level of living; living with my weaknesses but showing a greater power through them, and, indeed, because of them.

There is a basic condition for receiving that Higher Power, and that is a deep personal conviction that I need it. When the prodigal son 'came to his senses' (Lk 15:17) and said 'Oh my God, what a mess I'm in; and I'm in this mess because of *me*' he had taken the first major step towards recovery. The alcoholic's family and friends have been telling him for years, and then there comes a morning when he comes to his senses and sees what they

31

have seen all along. *Now* he is ready for that Higher Power.

'If anyone is in Christ he is a *new* creation; the old has gone, the new has come' (2 Cor 5:17). 'So from now on we regard no one from a worldly (external) point of view' (2 Cor 5:16). Paul himself had personal experience of the journey of conversion from external conformity to inner obedience. 'I was extremely zealous for the traditions of my fathers. But when God, who set me apart from birth and called me by his grace, was pleased to reveal his Son *in* me, so that I might preach him among the Gentiles, I did not consult any man . . . (Gal 1:14-16). His inner transformation was such that he could go on to say, 'I no longer live, but Christ lives in me . . . If righteousness could be gained through the law (external) then Christ died for nothing' (Gal 2:20-21). I must give one final quote from Paul on this whole area of inner power in the midst of human weakness. 'To keep me from becoming conceited because of these surpassing great revelations, there was given me a thorn in my flesh, a messenger of Satan, to torment me. Three times I pleaded with the Lord to take it away from me. But he said to me, "My grace is sufficient for you, for my power is made perfect in weakness." Therefore, I will boast all the more gladly about my weaknesses, so that Christ's power may rest on me. That is why, for Christ's sake, I delight in weaknesses . . . For when I am weak, then I am strong' (2 Cor 12:7-10).

CHAPTER SIX

Let your light shine

Let your light shine

If I did not have any human weaknesses Christ's power could not be witnessed through me. When, in spite of some personal weakness, I give evidence of a Higher Power overcoming and shining through that weakness – that is Christian witness. When I was deeply hurt, and have genuine and good reason never to forgive, and yet am seen to forgive – that is Christian witness. My grievance was real, and in a court of law I would win my case convincingly. But before the court of God the only victory is in witnessing to some aspect of love, which is God (1 Jn 4:16) – like forgiveness, tolerance, patience, sharing and caring.

We differ in our weaknesses, both in kind and in number. Therefore, we differ in our witness, and in the light that we are to others. 'You are the light of the world; . . . let *your* light shine before men that they may see your good deeds' (Mt 5:14-16). *Your* light is different from that of another, because your weaknesses are different. One person could be naturally very generous, while, if someone else was seen to be that way, it would be a seven-day wonder! The essence of Christian witness is what happens *after* there has been a change of heart. Only when it is evident that it must be the grace and power of God acting within, and not some natural goodness – only then is there genuine Christian witness. In the Living Bible paraphrased version of Paul's letter to the Galatians, Paul speaks of 'going to the Gentiles to *show* them the Good News about Jesus' (Gal 1:16). A Christian is in the business of *attracting* rather than *promoting*. People must *see* the light for themselves.

I remember speaking with some very confused young people recently. They had just returned from some sort of Pentecostal Rally, and after listening to several personal testimonies, they were wondering if it were necessary to hit skid row before one could meet Jesus! It seems each of the speakers had a tale of brokenness, sin, and despair before letting the Lord into their lives. This impression can, of course, be both dangerous and misleading. It is literally true that *every one* of us was lost until Jesus came into our lives, and without his spirit in our hearts we would be eternally lost. This is true even if, externally, we are nicer people with better morals, with a high level of human goodness and correct behaviour. The tendency, however, to stress, and sometimes overstress, the evidence of the rake and the wreck that has been redeemed and raised up is that the witness value is more evident. It can be more convincing, even if not necessarily more miraculous. On the other hand, Jesus found it much more difficult to touch the heart of a Pharisee than of a prostitute. In his eyes the witness of a change of heart in a Pharisee might have greater witness value, because it can be much more difficult to bring about.

Let your light shine. Your witness is essentially yours because that light must shine through your unique weaknesses. Conversion is something that is uniquely personal to each individual. Jesus took on *all* of human nature – which means, of course, that he also took on *my nature*. He does not *divide* his Spirit among his people. He offers me *all* of his Spirit for my unique personal struggles. I have my own personal cross, not made of wood. There are elements of Christian living and loving that I find are not really a burden at all, because I have a natural grace and facility in those areas. Of course, I know that even in these areas I do not have what it takes to *continue* living as I ought, without that Higher Power. With all the natural grace and goodness in the world the batteries (human energy) will run low and I will grind to a halt. There are other elements of Christian living that are just impossible for me, from the word 'go'. I just do not have what it takes. And then I get discouraged when I see others who have no struggle at all in those areas! I sometimes tend to overlook or forget the very things that are most important.

Someone said one time that to the fool every opportunity is a problem, but to the wise man every problem is an opportunity. Paul as much as said the same when he proclaimed that when he was weak then he was strong – 'because I can do all things through him who gives me strength' (Phil 4:13). I believe that the *real* confusion of my young friends earlier in this chapter is about the *content* of the witness. Is it a witness to how weak I am or how powerful God is? Christian witness is witnessing to God's power in me, and if others do not *see* this for themselves when they meet me, there is little point in telling them about it! Christian witness speaks for itself!

With Paul (Acts 13:47) we, too, can claim the promise in Isaiah as our own: 'I will make you a light for the Gentiles, that you may bring my salvation to the ends of the earth' (Is 47:6). *You* are the light of the world. Jesus first claimed that *he* was the light of the world (Jn 8:12). Then he told us that with his Spirit within us, *we* would be the light of the world (Mt 5:14). 'You will receive power when the Holy Spirit comes on you, and you will be my witnesses . . . to the ends of the earth' (Acts 1:8). Only when we have received the power can we give the witness. We cannot accept the privilege without accepting the responsibility. Jesus supplies the power and the light. In the words of St Francis, all I can hope for is to be a channel or an instrument of that power and of that light.

CHAPTER SEVEN

Satan as salesman

Satan as salesman

My weaknesses are not sin, but they can be sources of sin. God's power can shine out through our weaknesses, and indeed they are necessary for that power to be evidenced. Satan, however, knows our weaknesses and it is through those very same weaknesses that he tries to gain entry into our hearts. Satan is extremely clever and cunning, and he knows just how vulnerable we can be. He knows that without God's power, and our constant dependence and reliance on it, that we are at his mercy.

Because Satan knows our weaknesses, he can tailor his wares to ensure that his temptation is *really* tempting! He knows that a temptation for one person would not be a temptation for another, so there is a very personal and individual dimension to his approaches. He is, of course, 'a liar and the father of lies' (Jn 8:44), but he knows if my weaknesses include having an on-going struggle with truth! Jesus said that his Spirit was a Spirit of Truth to lead me into all truth (Jn 16:13), and would serve as an antidote to the poison of the Great Deceiver of God's people (Rev 12:9).

At the Last Supper Jesus told Peter, 'Simon, Simon, Satan has asked to sift you as wheat. But I have prayed for you, Simon, that your faith may not fail. And when you have turned back, strengthen your brothers' (Lk 22:31). Peter probably had this in mind when he himself tells us, 'Be alert . . . your enemy the devil prowls around like a roaring lion looking for someone to devour. Resist him, standing firmly in the faith, because you know that your brothers throughout the world are undergoing the same kind of sufferings' (1 Pet 5:8-9).

Satan is essentially a bully, and, like all bullies he will run away if we resist him and stand up to him, as Peter says. The greatest need we have is to be *filled* with the Spirit of God. The Spirit of evil can be overcome *only* by the Spirit of God. Jesus knows that trying to rid our hearts of the evil one, but not filling that vacuum with his Spirit is doomed to failure. 'When an evil spirit comes out of a man, it goes through arid places seeking rest and does not find it. Then it says, "I will return to the house I left!" When it arrives, it finds the house unoccupied, swept clean, and put in order. Then it goes off and takes with it seven other spirits more wicked than itself, and they go in and live there. And the final condition of that man is worse than the first' (Mt 12:43-45).

If I might compare my weaknesses to windows in a light-house. The light within wants to shine out through that glass, while the same light is drawing swarms of moths and flying insects of every kind, all trying to enter in where the light is shining out. Those insects are like the evil spirits, and Satan is the commander-in-chief of that army. The analogy breaks down, of course, if I take it one step further, and ask, what would happen if I switched off the light?! The insects would take themselves off elsewhere, whereas Satan and his army would move in to consolidate the darkness.

Jesus said, 'I have given you authority over all the power of the evil one' (Lk 10:19). In practice, that authority is his Holy Spirit. 'I write to you, young men, because you are strong, and the word of God lives in you, and you have overcome the evil one' (1 Jn 2:14). In other words, I have a spirit within me that is so much stronger than any evil spirit I could meet on the road of life. My biggest problem, perhaps, is not in having the power, but in forgetting that I have it. As long as I remember that power and act on it, Satan is kept in his place and has no power over me. 'Resist the devil, and he will flee from you' (Jas 4:7). 'For our struggle is not against flesh and blood, but against the rulers, against the authorities, against the power of this dark world, and against the spiritual forces of evil in the heavenly realms . . . Put on the full armour of God so that you can take your stand against the devil's schemes' (Eph 6:11-12).

When we refer to Satan and his methods of deception, then 'schemes' is a very apt word indeed! By myself I haven't a hope of out-manoeuvering him! If I know and accept my weaknesses, I have a much better chance of detecting the temptation. Every time I sin I have, once again, fallen for a lie. No sin of mine ever brought me happiness. I remember an alcoholic referring to many of the things that he did as being 'insane acts.' As he described them, I agreed with his conclusion. Many a time Satan can succeed in tricking us into irrational and indefensible behaviour. Jesus invites: 'I stand at the door and knock. If anyone hears my voice and opens the door, I will come in . . .' (Rev 3:20). 'Come to me all you who are burdened and heavy-laden and you will find rest' (Mt 11:28). Satan, on the other hand, bullies and is like the salesman who puts his foot in the doorway, and just won't go away! He *knows* that what he is offering is finding a *natural* response within us, and he will try anything to brow-beat, blackmail, and bulldoze his way into our hearts. Quite often the people he uses are among our closest friends, as he used Peter to try to distract and deter Jesus.

'Blessed is the man who perseveres under trial, because when he has stood the test, he will receive the crown of life that God has promised to those who love him . . . each one is tempted when, by his own evil desire, he is dragged away and enticed. Then, after desire has conceived, it gives birth to sin; and sin, when it is full-grown, gives birth to death. Don't be deceived, my dear brothers' (Jas 1:12,14-16). 'So, if you think you are standing firm, be careful that you don't fall! No temptation has seized you except what is common to man. And God is faithful; he will not let you be tempted beyond what you can bear. But when you are tempted, he will also provide a way out, so that you can stand up under it' (1 Cor 10:12-13).

CHAPTER EIGHT

The antidote

The antidote

Lucifer was amongst the most powerful and enlightened around the throne of God. Therefore, to rebel from such a position would be inexcusable and irrevocable. Whether it was love or hatred, it had to be very profound and immeasurably vast. There were no half-measures. It is even possible that his pride is such that he still believes he can defeat God!

When there is a poison there must be an antidote; where there is infection or a virus there must be an antibiotic. God created the perfect antidote for Satan's poison, and that is Mary. She is everything that Satan is not. She alone, as human nature's solitary beast, was born, lived, and died without any of our weaknesses or imperfections. This can be very puzzling to many people, because she then is seen as incapable of doing a *meritorious* act, because such goodness came naturally to her! This is a very valid question, and we must examine it for a while if we are to discover just where she fits in with our own struggles along the path of salvation.

Jesus, of his own free-will and personal decision *took on* the burden of our human weaknesses. It would be a whole different story had he inherited any of them, and had no choice! It would be a mistake to think of Mary as someone who just happened to be minding the house when Gabriel called! Oh no, she was a very deliberate and purposeful creation of God. Not only did humanity have to be saved from the grasp of Satan, but Satan himself had to be defeated. There is a very special touch of divine irony in this whole plan. God made Mary as the one single uncontaminated exception to the pollution of original sin. Mary was very, very unique in many ways. I believe she was so humble, so insignificant, and of such little consequence in her own eyes, in the eyes of the world, and even in the eyes of Satan, that he would never have considered her as the slightest threat to him, even if she did avoid the contamination of his lies! She was nothing – except in the eyes of God! 'God chose the foolish things of the world to shame the wise; God chose the weak things of the world to shame the strong. He chose the lowly things of the world, and the despised things – and the things that are not – to nullify the things that are, so that no one can boast before him!' (I Cor 1:27-30). For those whose 'mind is on earthly things' (Phil 3:20) Mary was of no consequence whatever.

Imagine Satan's horror, and complete viciousness when he learned that God was going to use this little insignificant back-woods girl as an essential element in crushing his head! Jesus himself would save us, and be our only Saviour; but in overcoming Satan, Mary as that divine antidote, would be God's trump card. This was the ultimate degradation for Satan, and he has an especial hatred for her and for her children (Rev 12:17). 'I will put enmity between you and the woman, and between your offspring and hers' (Gen 3:15), was God's verdict on Satan in the garden. Don't forget, Satan deceived Eve, and Eve was in a state of flawless humanity at the time. Even the most spotless and sinless human being is still limited, because 'human' implies limited, finite, mortal. Mary was *human,* and therefore heir to all the nuances of human living as distinct from human weaknesses. I myself believe that she was so empty of self that she was filled by God; 'full of grace' at the moment of annunciation; filled with the Spirit after that moment; and having the fullness of Christ from the moment of conception. Her strength was inner, and it was not her own. She was God's Trojan horse, as it were, through whom God himself entered into enemy territory and overcame that enemy. She was the one whom God used as an instrument for putting his plan of salvation into effect.

'There is but one mediator between God and man, Jesus Christ' (Heb 9:16). Mary is not Saviour, Redeemer, or Mediator, nor does she claim to be, or want to be. God could have overcome Satan totally without the co-operation or instrumentality of Mary. Jesus took on all of our human weaknesses and overcame them all through the power of the Spirit alone. Mary was that very deliberate and divinely inspired ingredient in God's rescue plan so that the pride, the arrogance, the aggression, and the destructive nature of Satan would be humiliated, deflated, and ultimately destroyed. Her example and the message of her life are just as valid as if she had to struggle with all of our human weaknesses. She, too, totally depended on the Spirit, and was totally open to that Spirit. Indeed, I could say that her claim to glory consists not so much in anything she herself did, but in allowing the Spirit of God full and total freedom to act in and through her. In this, she is a real and excellent example to all. Her advice is simple. She points to Jesus and says, 'Whatever he says you do' (Jn 2:5).

CHAPTER NINE

The miracle

The miracle

A miracle is not just something that I cannot do. There are many things that I cannot do and others can do with ease. A miracle is something that happens on the human level, in a human situation, that can only be done by the power of God. There are basic conditions needed for a miracle. The most fundamental condition is to accept the reality that the problem is beyond a human solution. Satan's pride is such that he would never admit defeat, or that he could not succeed in his determination to thwart God's plan and purpose for us. Because of his influence and effect, I, too, could have a latent hope that maybe, by myself, I could succeed! I know that Jesus said that without him I can do nothing, and apart from him I can do nothing, (Jn 15:4-5), but I don't always take that as literally as Jesus meant it.

Look at some scenes in the Gospel. Jairus did what he could for his daughter, and the centurion did all he could for his servant. The Apostles baled the water from the sinking boat, and Peter cast out his nets again and again. There came that moment, however, when it just had to be accepted and acknowledged that all efforts were ending in failure, and future efforts seemed doomed to failure. Each person had to acknowledge the truth of the situation with these or similar words or thoughts, 'I have done all I can do, and I have failed. I just give up, because it is obvious by now that there is nothing more I can do.' There we have a primary step in procuring a miracle.

The next step for Jairus, the centurion, or the apostles, was to turn to someone who *could* do something about their situation. They had to be as sure and certain of this conclusion as they were of the first one. They turned to Jesus, because they *knew* that he could do something about their predicament. Added to that conviction was the certainty that he *would* do it, because he cared enough to *want* to. They went to him, or called out to him, and Jesus knew from their whole approach that they had the basic conditions for a miracle. Jairus 'came and fell at Jesus' feet, pleading with him to come to his house because his only daughter, a girl of twelve, was dying' (Lk 8:41-42). The conditions are all there in that sentence.

I myself struggled for many years before I came to the conclusion that I, too, needed a miracle! I can change the furniture in my room, can change my appearance, can change my name – but I cannot change my heart. That can only be done by the power of God. That requires a miracle. In the account of Creation we are told that 'the Lord God formed man from the dust of the ground, and breathed into his nostrils the breath of life and man became a living being' (Gen 2:7). The shaping of the form of clay was well within human competence, but the instilling of life and the bringing to life required the power of God. When that inner life was contaminated by original sin, there was need for a new creation, for another miracle. 'For they who are in Christ become a new creation; the old has gone, the new has come!' (2 Cor 5:17). With the psalmist we must cry out to the Lord, 'Create in me a pure heart, O God, and renew a steadfast spirit within me' (Ps 51:10). To create or to recreate is the work of a Creator, not of a creature.

There is great stress to-day on various methods of psychotherapy, on self-help groups, and on group dynamics. These all have a part to play, of course, but when it comes to a change of heart, to an inner renewal, they are limited, and very finite. They serve a purpose when they help to heighten the good-will, and the inner

51

discernment. There is no way, however, that I can by-pass the miracle if I need permanent change. The most they can do is some sort of maintenance job that may tide me over until the next crisis. The tape-recorder with batteries will play, of course, but it will not last; it will run down. The tape-recorder that is plugged into a power socket will maintain an on-going ability to function.

Jesus speaks of his peace, not the peace the world gives, which is fragile and limited (Jn 14:27). He offers abundant life, joy pressed down and flowing over (Jn 17:13), and he reminded us, 'You did not choose me, but I have chosen you; and I have appointed you to go and bear fruit – *fruit that will last*' (Jn 15:16). Only the divine can provide the quality that enables something to last. *Eternal* is one of the divine attributes.

In my struggle with my human weaknesses, I encounter a lot of failure. I can look back down the road I have travelled and see it littered and strewn with broken promises, reneged decisions, and unfulfilled intentions. So much for human endeavour, and for muscular Christianity! These are not really failures, of course, if I learn the obvious lesson from them – and then turn to a Higher Power.

It is important to remind ourselves that there will always be a struggle, because I am not perfect, and must not ask the Lord *to take away* my weaknesses. I need them, and without them there can be no authentic Christian witness. To be saved means to have a Saviour, to have a Higher Power, to have a dependable map for the journey of life back home to the Father. On any journey I encounter sign-posts, traffic lights, and road signs. These don't *do* anything nor do they compel *me* to do anything. I must acknowledge them, advert to them, and obey them. All those broken promises and reneged decisions, that are strewn along my road of life so far, are evidence of disobedience, of singing my own song ('I did it my Way') or of writing my own story ('Going my way')!

So vital is the conviction of my need for a miracle, that to arrive at that conviction is itself a miracle! So endemic is our pride and self-sufficiency that we will either struggle along from failure to disaster, and blame the whole world, or else decide that we're born losers anyhow, and just give up the struggle. That is why the conviction of the need for a miracle is such a unique grace. When I cry out, 'My God, I need something!' It implies that I myself don't have it! 'You see, at just the right time, when we were still powerless, Christ died for us' (Rom 5:6). It is just when we are helpless and powerless that Jesus makes available to us the help and the power that we need.

CHAPTER TEN

Incarnation

Incarnation

God does not change. Jesus is the same yesterday, today, and always' (Heb 13:8). God is Creator, and he just won't turn around and become a destroyer. If this world is in the process of being destroyed then the credit (or blame) belongs to us. God is love. He loves you, and could not *ever* not love you. Even if someone ended up in hell, God's love has not changed. By a fundamental option in life, that person put himself outside of the arc of God's love. Does that mean that God's love is limited, and can only stretch a certain length? No, it means that his love is such a generous and feeling love that he does not in any way try to manipulate or coerce a response from me. He gives me total freedom to say 'no' to his love, and to put myself outside that love.

Compared to human beings and human endeavour which must change and ultimately come to an end, God and the ways of God have an unchanging and eternal quality to them. God's love for us was expressed in a tangible, visible way when he sent his only begotten Son (Jn 3:16). God's plan in making this possible was through the co-operation of Mary with his Holy Spirit. That plan was successful, and God sees no reason to change it!

Incarnation is ongoing. I said in an earlier chapter that the Holy Land is in my heart. It is there that I must have my Nazareth, Bethlehem, Calvary and Upper Room. The Incarnation has to take place in me, and God's way of effecting this is still through the co-operation of Mary with the Holy Spirit. When that Incarnation becomes a reality within me, then with Paul I can say, 'I live now, not I, but Christ lives in me' (Gal 2:20). Mary's role is one of co-operating, of facilitating. It is the Spirit who is the dynamic or active force. Not that Mary is or ever was totally passive, not more than I myself can afford to be. It is the motherly instinct in her that will cultivate my co-operation with her, and make Incarnation possible.

Incarnation is the miracle I wrote about in the last chapter – nothing more, nothing less. To put it that way is surely to hold it up as something above and beyond my competence. As I put the drop of water in the wine at Mass, I pray that I 'may come to share in the *divinity* of Christ, who humbled himself to share in our humanity'. I can only ask for this, pray for this, long for this – and expect this.

When Jesus took on all of human nature, he took on all of mine. His work in me and his plan for me must be brought to completion. 'Not that I have already obtained all this, or have already been made perfect, but I press on to take hold of that for which Christ Jesus took hold of me. I do not consider myself yet to have taken hold of it. But one thing I do: forgetting what is behind, and straining towards what is ahead, I press on towards the goal to win the prize for which God has called me heavenwards in Christ Jesus' (Phil 3:12-14). Even with the inner miracle of Incarnation, I must 'press on' and struggle ahead. Jesus himself *was* Incarnation, and 'He still did not cling to equality with God' (Phil 2:6), and never looked for easy options.

The Spirit of God is given to us, not to make things *easy,* but to make things *possible.* The struggle against our weaknesses, and the forces of evil that 'capitalise' on such weaknesses is the very essence of Christian living and of Incarnation. The struggle doesn't abate or disappear, but my approach and attitude towards that struggle will be utterly changed. Putting the drop of water in the wine at Mass symbolises my joining forces with Christ in walking the same road, in the power of the same Spirit. It is a daily prayer for Incarnation and a daily commitment to it.

Paul was clear and to the point when he spoke to the early Christians about the nature of their calling. 'My dear children, for whom I am again in the pains of childbirth until *Christ is formed in you*' (Gal 4:19). 'And I pray that you may be filled with *the fullness of God*' (Eph 3:19). Peter and John were no less unambiguous. 'His divine power has given us everything we need for life and godliness . . . so that you may participate in *the Divine nature*' (2 Pet 1:3-4). 'No one who is *born of God* will continue to sin, because God's seed remains in him; he cannot go on sinning, because he has been born of God' (1 Jn 3:9).

CHAPTER ELEVEN

Supervising the miracle

Supervising the miracle

The co-operation of Mary with the Holy Spirit within me is what enables Incarnation to take place. Mary is best seen, then, as the housekeeper of my heart. It is she who provides an openness to the Spirit by turning my heart into a prayer room, an Upper Room. In my case, the Incarnation follows on my Pentecost. She is the one who supervises the miracle of the heart.

Quite often the human heart can become a problem room, where I can brood, and wallow in self-pity and self-deception. I can surface from there with depression and bitterness. It is Mary of Cana who can obtain and supervise the miracle of change from the insipid waters of human limitation to the 'best wine' of divine life. Mary did, in a beautiful way, what I am called on to do. And yet, in a way, it can be said that it was not a question of what she herself did, but in what she allowed the Spirit to do in her. Once again, I stress that it is the Spirit who acts, and it is Christ who is formed, but Mary is the beautiful and essential catalyst in the process of conversion and of change.

Mary is God's antibiotic for the virus and infection of Satan. She is essentially a person of the heart. 'But as for Mary, she treasured these words, and pondered them in her heart' (Lk 2:19). Not only does she point to Jesus with the words, 'Do whatever he tells you' (Jn 2:15), but she helps me hear, understand and respond to what he says. Padre Pio never had any doubt that it was Mary who taught him the secrets of suffering and of Eucharist. She was the Novice Mistress of his heart, and she supervised his formation. Incarnation became so real in him that, much to his confusion and embarrassment, the presence of Christ was evidenced externally as well! He may have felt that she did too good a job!

When Jesus spoke of 'becoming like little children' (Mt 18:3), he might well have been thinking of his mother. Little boys cling to their mothers, depend on them, and turn to them in all their needs. Then when they come to 'the awkward age', as they move from the dependent stage to the independent stage, the poor mother can become an embarrassment! I have known boys who would not want their pals to see them in town with their mothers! They will tag nonchalantly well to the rear, or even try the opposite footpath! It is, indeed, an awkward age, because their struggling towards independence can make dependence intolerable. They cannot yet distinguish between child-likeness and child-ishness.

The same can happen to us in our relationship with Mary. We can boast of our preferences to go straight to the Source! Had we been at Cana we would have asked Jesus ourselves! Peter may have had a real problem with Mary, as he had with the other mothers! However, when he had fallen on his face at the approach of Calvary, and then lifted his eyes and saw that she still stood there with Jesus (Jn 19:26), he was more prepared and willing to allow her take charge of the Upper Room!

A mother is directly involved in the procreation of new life. She is also directly involved in the on-going creation and development, and is the first and primary teacher of her child. She supervises and assists in the early learning process. That learning process, of necessity, involves mistakes, set-backs, and discouragement. Her mother's heart provides the gentle coaching and coaxing that are essential at that stage. In a way, she has to work towards redundancy, and she is only successful when her child can walk alone, and his children after him.

Paul calls our inner growth 'learning to live and to walk in the Spirit' (Gal 5:16). We need a spiritual mother to supervise and encourage us on this journey – and we have one, Jesus said, 'I will not leave you orphans' (Jn 14:18), and then he gave me his Father and his Mother. It would be a great pity if a spirit of childish independence led me to opt for a one-parent family! I remember my own deep personal joy and satisfaction every time I heard someone pay compliments to my own mother. I didn't feel slighted, lessened, or detracted from in any way! I would readily accept that Jesus loved his Mother more than I love mine! Suggesting that giving Mary a place in my journey of life would belittle the place of Jesus, is simply not true, and I fail to see how it could possibly be pleasing to the Lord.

Making Mary the housekeeper of my heart is not just a nice pious idea! It must be literal and for real. Faith is not just mental assent, whereby I agree with something and acknowledge it to be truth. It is a conviction of the heart, on which I *act*. The *idea* of Mary being the housekeeper may be in the head for a long long time, before it becomes a reality in the heart. The journey from the head to the heart is a long journey indeed, and it is really only effected through prayer. The kind of prayer that is needed is not so much *words* as a constant and continual desire and longing. It is a sort of inner hunger, because God always 'fills the hungry with good things' (Lk 1:53), as Mary assures us.

Mary combined the active and the contemplative dimensions of Christian living in a very remarkable way. She pondered and cherished the word in the quiet of her heart, and then when she met Elizabeth, Simeon, Anna and the Shepherds, or the Wise Men, she presented that Word to them. That is what she wishes to supervise in my heart. She can turn on the faucet of the Spirit when I pray, or she can be with me at weddings or other gatherings when the well can run dry, and she is alert to the situation. If she herself did not have to struggle with human weaknesses, then she certainly wants to share in my struggle. Imagine the warmth of the welcome in the home if Mary answered your ring at the front door. There is always a warmth and a welcome for Jesus, even when disguised as 'the least of the brethren', when Mary is the housekeeper of the heart.

And finally, gentle reader, you who have accompanied me on the journey from the first chapter where one mother was making bread, to the last chapter, where another mother is the housekeeper of my heart, I do hope you recognised yourself here and there along the way. I need hardly remind you that whatever weaknesses you had before you began this book, you still have them all at the end! But I hope you have something more, much more. I hope that together we can end with this simple prayer:

Dear Lord,
please leave me with my weaknesses and imperfections,
so that the Power of your Spirit
may be clearly evident in me.
May that Spirit touch the hearts of those I meet,
either through the words I say,
the prayers I pray,
the life I live,
or the person that I am.
God bless you.